Contents

...er, c. 1790

At the supermarket

Amy went to the supermarket with her Granny.
Amy pushed the trolley.

Granny bought enough food for a week.
She bought fresh food, tinned food and
frozen food.

She paid for it all at the check-out.

Granny said, "When I was first married there were no supermarkets.

I went shopping every day.
There were no frozen foods.

The shopkeeper served everyone and wrapped up the goods."

Laxton, 1952

At school Amy's class made a shop.

Amy told the class about shopping when Granny was young.

Their teacher Miss Stirling said, "How can we find out about shopping in the past?"

"Look at books in the school library," said Tom.

"Ask someone old," said Amy.

"Look in a museum," said Sanjit.

Markets

They found some pictures of markets in the school library.

Market stalls are the oldest kind of shops.
Some towns have had a weekly market
for hundreds of years.

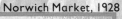

Norwich Market, 1928

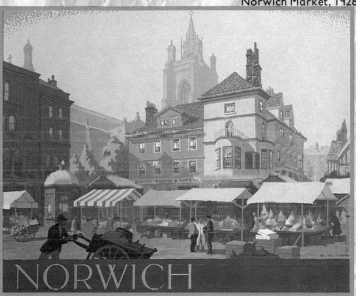

Old Fishmarket, Norwich, early 19th century

Which of these pictures is old?

Which one is very old?

Catalogues

Tom's Mum buys things from a catalogue. People have been shopping like this for about a hundred years.

Here is a page from an old catalogue. It was sent out about eighty years ago. Look at the boy's clothes. Do boys dress like this today?

Army and Navy Catalogue, 1913

Here is a page from a new catalogue. You can buy the goods by joining a shopping club. Then you only have to make a small payment each week.

Kays Catalogue, 1989

Most people buy things from shops.
This picture shows a grocer's shop
about two hundred years ago.

Glasgow shopkeeper, c. 1790

It sold lemons, candles and
tea from a green tin.

The pointed packets are sugar loaves.
Sugar used to be sold in hard blocks.
In this shop they have been wrapped
in sugar paper.
The shopkeeper had a cutter like this
to break the sugar up.

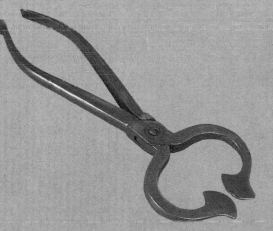

What do you think might have been
kept in the green drawers?

Here is a picture of Sainsbury's in 1906.

Customers had to queue twice if they wanted to buy things from each counter.

Sometimes they sat on chairs while they waited for their groceries to be weighed and packed.

Sainsbury's, Croydon, 1950

The first supermarkets opened
about forty years ago.
This shop was new in 1950.

Shopkeepers thought people would
buy more if they could pick up things
for themselves.
Customers liked it because it was
quicker and they could see all the
goods for sale.

Forty years ago new kinds of goods
were put on sale.
This shop is selling frosted food.

What do we call it today?

Leicester, 1950

Shop signs

Amy's class looked at the pictures very carefully.
They talked about what they could see.

Here is an old photo of a shopping street.
The shops are all quite small.

Cirencester, 1903

The shopkeepers often lived over the shop. They hung things outside to show people what they sold.

Here are some old shop signs.
Can you tell what each shop sold?

Glasgow, c. 1924

Shop windows were smaller in the past. People hadn't found out how to make very large sheets of glass.

Shopkeepers made their windows look nice so that people would come in and buy.

Advertisement for Fry's chocolate, c. 1905

Next the class found some pictures of old advertisements.
They showed what people could buy in the past.

Can we buy any of these things today?

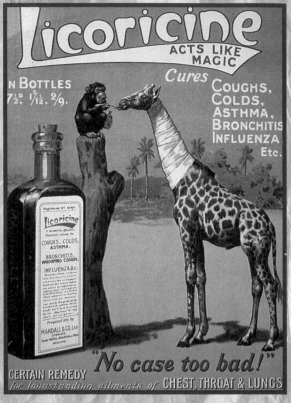

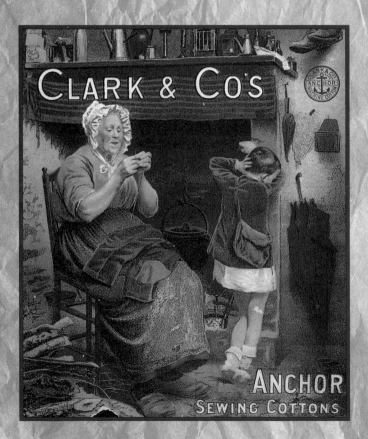

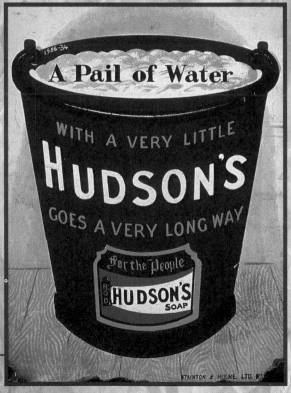

Amy's class asked people about shopping in the past.

Tom's Grandad said that some shops used to make the things they sold.
He could just remember a basket maker's shop when he was young. The baskets were made in the workshop at the back and sold to the customers in the shop at the front.

Can you think of any shops where they still make the things they sell?

Market Hill, Cambridge, c. 1900

When Amy's Grandad was young he
delivered meat for the butcher.
He said, "Shops used to deliver more
things then than they do today."

April 1937

Hand milk cart, c. 1920

What was delivered by this bike,
this handcart and this van?

Morris Minor Van, 1936

Tom asked his Granny about shopping when she was a girl. She said, "Things were put in paper bags not plastic ones. Sometimes they were wrapped up and tied with string."

Here is an old egg box and a packet of tea.

"Biscuits came in huge tins and the shopkeeper weighed out as many as you wanted.
At Christmas there were special small tins. This money box had biscuits in it when it was given to me as a present."

Sanjit's family run a grocer's shop. They sell Indian food.
He said, "People like to buy food from abroad.
In the past we could only sell dried food but now
there are aeroplanes we can sell fresh food as well."

This is a Jewish grocer's shop. It sells the kind
of food that Jewish people like to eat.

There are tins of pickles on the top shelf,
sausages hanging from the ceiling and
smoked salmon in the boxes on the counter.

Sanjit's neighbour Miss Townend showed him some of the things she had kept from her parents' clothes shop.
She had a bag,
a string cutter,
a hat stretcher and
a tool for measuring
the size of hats.

Hat stretcher

String cutter

Hat measure

Miss Townend said, "Everything was kept in drawers behind the counter.

We measured people for everything, even their hats and gloves.

We had models in the window to show the clothes."

At the museum

Amy's class went to the museum to find out more about shopping. The museum teacher showed them a doll dressed as a pedlar.

She said, "Pedlars travelled from door to door selling useful things from their baskets."

What is the pedlar doll selling?

Next they saw a painting of a pedlar. She was selling china.

They saw some of the same china in a glass case.

Pedlar woman doll, 1820–1830

A pedlar by Myles Birket Foster, c. 1873

The museum had an old cash till. It had a drawer which opened when you pulled the handle.

It stored the money safely and the customer could see the cost of each sale.

Miss Stirling said, "It's all in pounds, shillings and pence. That was the money we used before 1971 when we changed to decimal money.
There were twenty shillings in a pound and twelve pennies in a shilling."

"Five pounds is the highest amount on the till," said Tom.

"A farthing is the smallest amount," said Miss Stirling. "It was a quarter of a penny."

Here are some old price labels in shillings and pence.

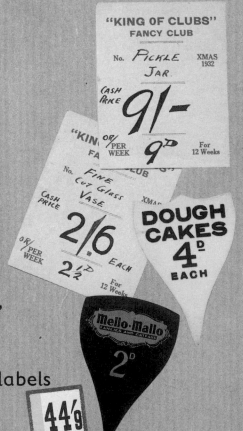

Next they saw the old shop in the museum.

These old packets have been collected
by the museum and put on show to
look like an old shop.

'The General Store' from Buckley's Shop Museum, Battle, Sussex

They saw how tea
was weighed in the
scales and wrapped
in a paper parcel.

Miss Stirling said,
"Shops don't need
scales so much
nowadays. Most
things are weighed
and packed in the
factory."

They looked at all the packets, jars and
tins on the shelves.

They pointed at things we
can still buy today.

On the way home the class saw an old corner shop that had just closed down.

Miss Stirling said, "People don't go to small shops so much nowadays. They go to supermarkets and big department stores. They can buy everything they need in the same building.

Supermarkets usually have car parks so that you don't have to carry your shopping home."

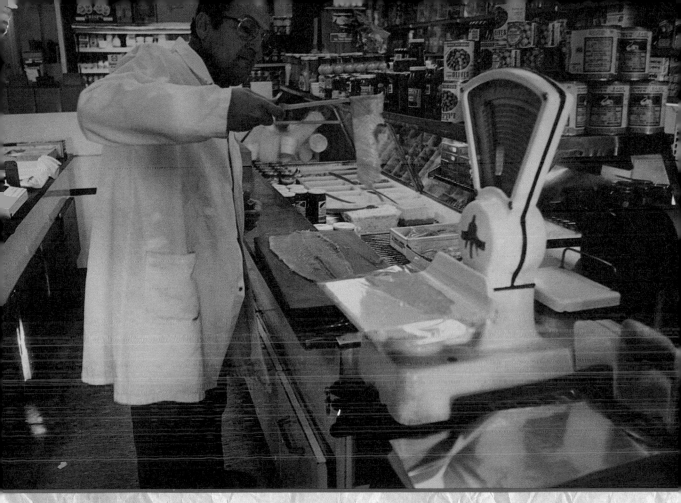

Amy said that her Mum often buys things at the corner shop.

"It's close to our house and it stays open late.
It's very useful if you forget to buy everything
you need at the supermarket."

Sanjit said that his parents' shop is always busy.

"We sell things that you can't always get at
the supermarket."

Miss Stirling asked the class if they thought that corner shops
would survive in the future. What do you think?

Back at school Amy's class decided to make
their own collection of packets, labels and bags.

They stuck them all in a scrapbook and
put it in the school library so that children
at school in the future would know what
shopping was like today.